My First

Islamic Book

for Children under 3

Copyright © 2020 by Julia Hanke
All rights reserved
Printed by **AMAZON**

Illustrator: Sarah Mahmoud

As Salamu Alaykum, Dear Readers,

As Muslim parents, we all want one thing for our children: provide an authentic Islamic education. We want our children to grow up with good Islamic morals, manners, behavior, and values. The problem I encountered as a homeschooling mother of three children, age 8, 5, and 1 is the following: The Islamic books for children I found and bought for my children are either lacking in authenticity, are written in a language that is too complicated for children, or they hardly contain valuable content. The content is so low that my children would learn almost nothing new.

This is why I wrote this book: "My first Islamic Book for Children under 3." It provides rich content with valuable information Muslim children need to grow into pious, well-mannered, and well-behaved, kind human beings.

The stories are real stories taken straight from popular, authentic Islamic sources like Tafsir Ibn Kathir and the Hadith books of Bukhari and Muslim. I simplified the language so that these stories are easy to understand, even for young children aged two and above. When I wrote the book, my oldest son was two and a half, and he would understand everything well alhamdulillah, but it still depends on your child's language skills.

As a holder of a B.A. in Education and Islamic Sciences, I understand how important it is to use authentic Islamic sources when teaching our children. This is what was especially important to me, so I was passionate about writing this book. The facial features of the Illustrations have recently been removed from the print version of the book to adhere to the Islamic prohibition of drawing pictures of animate beings. Don't let your child miss out on essential and nurturing Islamic education. Grab a copy for your relatives and friends, and share the joy of learning!

Thank you for purchasing this book! If you enjoy it, I would be very grateful if you posted a short review on Amazon. Your support does make a difference and I read every review personally. Since the book is printed by Amazon please note that I, as the author, have no influence on the print quality. Please contact Amazon's customer service for any printing related issues. Thank you for your understanding!

CONTENTS

CONTENTS

Allah's Names

and their meanings for our daily lives

The greatest name
Allah

Allah is the greatest name of our Creator. But Allah has many other names as well, which refers to His many qualities. The Prophet Muhammed (peace and blessings of Allah be upon him) used Allah's other names in different situations, for example, before eating or leaving the house.

2

Whenever we start a good activity, we are told to start it in the name of Allah. So before we pray, or eat, go to the bathroom, or leave the house to go somewhere, we should say "Bismillah."

3

Bismillah means "with the name of Allah," so by saying this, we are saying that we want to do all of our actions for Allah to make Him happy. That helps us keep Allah in our minds, so we can be thankful and be aware that He is watching us, so we do not do bad things, and lastly, it is a way to ask Allah for His protection. We call on Allah by taking His name to say "Allahumma," which means "Oh Allah." Many duas start with "Allahumma," like the prayer before we sleep, the prayer when we wake in the morning, and the prayer for protection.

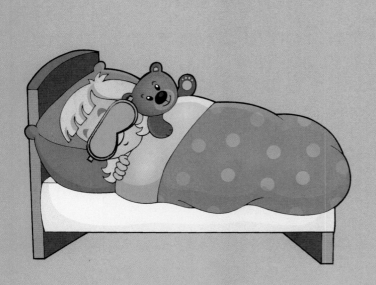

4

Al Wahid and Al Ahad

Allah has two more names similar in their meaning – Al Wahid and Al Ahad. Al Wahid means The One and Al Ahad means The Unique. When we call on Allah by those names, we remember that Allah is the origin of all life, and He is the only God. He is perfect. We have to do all kinds of worship (prayer, dua, fasting) for Him Alone. Nothing and no one is like Him. He is unique.

Ar-Rahman and Ar-Raheem (The Most Gracious and The Most Merciful)

Two of Allah's names that you hear lots are Ar Rahman and Ar Raheem. You probably remember hearing them following "Bismillah." They mean The Most Gracious and the Most Merciful. To get an idea of how merciful Allah is, we are taught that Allah divided all the mercy in the universe into 100 parts. He sent down one of those parts to humankind, jinn, animals, and wildlife, for all of creation to use to be merciful to each other so that we see even wild animals being kind to their babies.

6

7

The rest, 99 parts, He kept for Himself, which He uses to be merciful to His slaves on the Day of Judgement. If you look at the creation, you can see beautiful examples of Allah's Mercy. Have you ever seen a Mummy horse lifting her leg when the foal (baby horse) is drinking from her udder (breasts) so that her baby doesn't get hurt?

The lions eat the young of other animals, but they don't eat their cubs because of this mercy. Imagine that there have been so many people and animals, and each of them has used so much mercy in their lives, and yet add it all up, and it's still only a tiny part compared to what Allah has for us. He truly is The Most Merciful.

9

Mercy is such a beautiful quality that the Prophet Muhammed (peace and blessing of Allah be upon him) said: "Whoever does not show mercy to others will not receive mercy." It means that whoever is not kind to others will not get kindness and mercy from Allah. We should try our best to be kind and merciful to other people, Muslims and non-Muslims, adults, children, and even animals and plants.

Al Mo'men (The Bestower of Security)

Allah is Al Mo'men – the bestower of security. Whenever you are scared of something, for example if you are scared of the darkness, ask Allah by His name Al Mo'men to protect you from harm. He is the only one who can truly protect you. If He wills, no one can hurt you.

When we ask Allah to keep us safe, we should make sure that others around us are safe as well. This includes our families, brothers and sisters, our neighbors, our friends, and all people Muslim or non–Muslim. The Prophet Muhammad (peace and blessing of Allah be upon him) said: "One whose neighbor is not safe from his harm will not enter paradise."

Looking after our neighbors is very important. It means to not shout or be loud when the neighbors are sleeping. We should respect their property and not leave our toys or rubbish in their gardens or shared hallways. And we should always offer them a smile as a charity. Giving security to others also means not hurting our families. We should be kind to our brothers and sisters, even if they annoy us. We should not fight with them or be mean. And we should respect and obey our parents and not cause them stress by being rude or disobedient.

14

Al Muhaymin (The Watcher)

Allah is Al Muhaymin – The Watcher – which should remind us that He can see us, so we should make good choices instead of bad ones. Remembering that Allah is Al Muhaymin should also lead us to Ihnsan. What is "Ihnsan"? The Prophet Muhammad (peace and blessings of Allah be upon him) said: "Ihnsan is to worship Allah as if you see Him and if you can't see Him, indeed He sees you."

I will not sneak the chocolate from the fridge. Allah can see me!

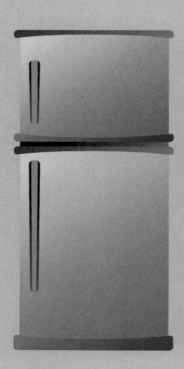

15

If we can feel that Allah is watching us, we will always do the best we can to be good. Also, the Prophet (peace and blessings of Allah be upon him) said: "Allah loves from each and every one of us that if we do anything we do it to our best of our ability." It means that whenever we do something, we do the best we can. If we are aware that Allah is watching us and knows what we are thinking, we should also try to stop ourselves from thinking bad because that might cause us to act badly or talk in a bad language.

Al Aziz (The Mighty)

Allah is also Al Aziz– The Mighty. This name of Allah means that Allah has the most power and strength of all. Nothing and no one can overpower Him. Allah cannot be forced to do anything. Allah is powerful that only if He wills, something will happen. If He doesn't want it to happen, no one can make it happen. The Pharaoh of Prophet Musa's time had to learn this the hard way when he tried to hurt all the baby boys of the Banu Israel because he knew that a boy would be born from the Banu Israel who will, later on, destroy his kingdom. Allah made sure that Prophet Musa, known in English as "Moses" peace be upon him, who was a boy from the Banu Israel, was kept safe.

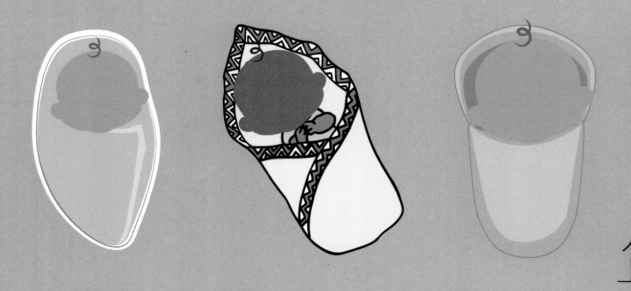

17

Allah made it so that Pharaoh himself looked after the very child who would take his power away from him later. Baby Musa was put in a basket on the Nile River to keep him safe from the Pharaoh's soldiers and was found by the Pharaoh's wife, who decided to take him to the palace and look after him as if he would be her child. That is the power of Al Aziz.

18

Two similar names to Al Aziz are Al Qawee, which means the Strong, and Al Mateen, The Powerful. These names also show how strong Allah is. Allah is so strong; He could pick up all the cars in the whole world!

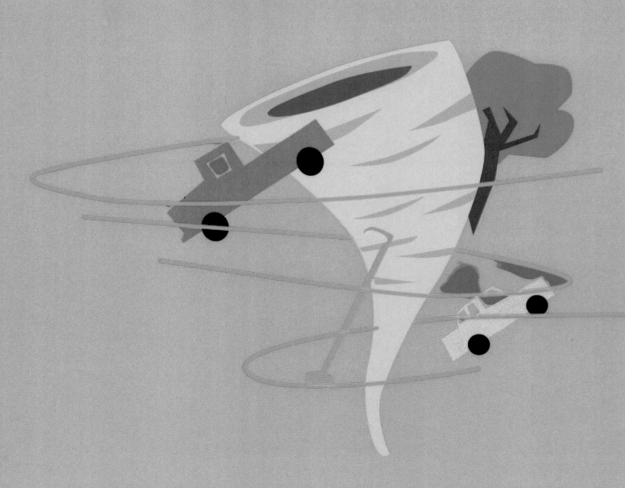

19

Allah is the one that controls the winds, the water and waves, and the thunder and lightning. Another similar name is Al Qadeer, which means the All-Powerful and Able. This name reveals that Allah can do everything He wants. When He wants a thing to be, He just says 'Be!' and it is.

20

Al Kabeer

Allah is Al Kabeer. He is greater and bigger than everything. We cannot even understand Allah completely because our knowledge is not big enough for that. That's why we don't ask how Allah is or where He came from, or what He looks like. Allah has a hand, but we don't ask how it looks like. Allah has a face, but we don't ask how it looks like because we cannot imagine it. There is also a hadith in which the Prophet (peace and blessings of Allah be upon him) tells us that every night, Allah comes down to the lowest heaven, the one where the moon, the stars, and the planets are.

The Prophet (peace and blessings of Allaah be upon him) said: "The Lord descends every night to the lowest heaven when one-third of the night remains and says: 'Who will call upon Me, that I may answer Him? Who will ask of Me, that I may give him? Who will seek My forgiveness, that I may forgive him?'" This continues until dawn (until Fajr). This hadith of the Prophet Muhammad (peace and blessings of Allaah be upon him) should encourage us to make a lot of dua in that last third of the night. We believe that Allah comes down to the lowest heaven every night, but we don't ask how He does it.

22

As Samee' (The All Hearing)

Allah is As Samee', which means The All Hearing. He can hear everything we say and everything we think even if we don't say it out loud. Even when we are whispering or saying something so quietly that no one else can hear it, Allah can hear it. He can hear the tiniest voice and the quietest whisper. Allah heard Prophet Yunus' dua from inside the belly of a whale fish.

23

Ar Razaq (The Provider)

Allah is Ar Razaq, which means The Provider. He provides food, drink, clothes, money, and housing for all the world's people, even non–Muslims. The non–Muslims do not thank Allah much, and they don't listen to Allah, but Allah is still providing for them. Allah even provides food and drink for all the animals. They do not have jobs, but they manage to find the food and water they need to survive!

Al Baseer (The All Seeing)

Allah is Al Baseer, The All–Seeing. He can see everything. Allah can see a small black ant crawling over a black stone in the blackest night. He can see the fish and other animals swimming in the deep and dark water. He can see us even if we are hiding in a cave or in a place where no one else can see us. He can see us no matter where we are.

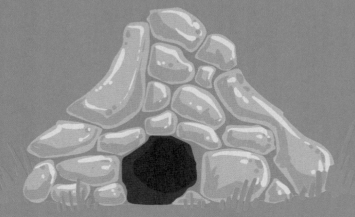

25

Al Aleem (The All Knower)

Allah is Al Aleem, which means The All-Knowing. The Quran says: "And with Him are the keys of the Ghaib (all that is hidden), none knows them but He. And He knows whatever there is in the earth and in the sea; not a leaf falls, but He knows it..." [6:59]

26

Allah knows how many leaves are falling from the trees, how much rain will fall, and when. He knows what we are thinking and what we will be thinking about tomorrow and which decisions we will make. Allah knows how many birds are flying in the sky and how many stars there are because He created everything. He made them all.

Al Quddoos (The Holy)

Allah is Al Quddoos, The Holy. It means He is free of any defects. He never makes a mistake. Allah is perfect. Only we humans make mistakes and sin. That's one reason why nothing and no one can be like Allah. He is perfect, and no one is even close to being like Him.

28

As Salaam (The Peace)

Another name of Allah is As-Salaam, which means The Giver of Peace. Peace is a very important thing in Islam. That is why when we greet each other, we say "Assalamu 'Alaikum" or "peace be upon you." If someone welcomes you with "Assalamu 'Alaikum," you have to reply, "Wa 'alaikum Salam." This should be said with a smile.

29

As Samad (The Self-Sufficient)

Allah is As Samad, which means The Self Sufficient. Being self-sufficient means, He does not need anyone or anything. He can sustain Himself. He is the only one who can do that. All people, animals, jinn, everything, and everyone needs Allah to survive. Allah gives us these very important things like air to breathe, food, water, sunshine, energy to move and play, and even help or friendship. But Allah is so strong, and so complete, that He does not need anyone or anything. We need Allah, but Allah does not need us. He does not need food, water, air, or sleep.

30

Good Habits

Say "Alhamdulillah" when you wake up

Bath or shower regularly

Cover your mouth and nose when you sneeze

31

Throw your rubbish in the bin

Put your toys away after playing with them

Say "Jazak Allahu Khairan" when someone gives you a gift

Knock before you enter somebody's room

Say "Bismillah" before you eat

Don't talk to strangers

Say "Alhamdulillah" after you finished eating

33

When you knock into somebody by accident, say "Sorry".

Listen to your parents and be kind to them

Be quite when someone is praying

34

One last thing - I would love to hear your feedback about this book! If you enjoyed this book or found it useful, I would be very grateful if you posted a short review on Amazon. Your support does make a difference and I read every review personally.

You can also sign up with your e-mail address on:

www.islamicbooks.shop

to find out when new books are being released and get FREE audiobooks, e-books, and other educational resources! I am still looking for reviewers for my new book about anger management in Islam for children age 5 and above.

Made in the USA
Las Vegas, NV
10 January 2021